SELECTIONS FROM

100 GREATEST SONGS of ROCK & ROLL

1 VH
Music First

CLARINET

Available for

FLUTE, CLARINET, ALTO SAX, TENOR SAX, TRUMPET, HORN, TROMBONE, VIOLIN, VIOLA, CELLO

The following songs have been omitted from this publication because of licensing restrictions:

Johnny B. Goode
Jumpin' Jack Flash
Kashmir
Rock and Roll
Sympathy for the Devil
Whole Lotta Shakin' Goin' On

ISBN 978-1-4803-4132-6

HAL•LEONARD® CORPORATION

7777 W. BLUEMOUND RD. P.O. BOX 13819 MILWAUKEE, WI 53213

Visit Hal Leonard Online at
www.halleonard.com

ALL ALONG THE WATCHTOWER

CLARINET

Words and Music by
BOB DYLAN

ALL SHOOK UP

Clarinet

Words and Music by OTIS BLACKWELL
and ELVIS PRESLEY

AMERICAN PIE

CLARINET

Words and Music by
DON McLEAN

D.S. al Coda

CODA

BEAT IT

CLARINET

Words and Music by
MICHAEL JACKSON

Moderately fast

BLOWIN' IN THE WIND

CLARINET

Words and Music by
BOB DYLAN

Moderately, in 2

BLUE SUEDE SHOES

CLARINET

Words and Music by
CARL LEE PERKINS

BORN TO BE WILD

Clarinet

Words and Music by
MARS BONFIRE

BOHEMIAN RHAPSODY

CLARINET

Words and Music by
FREDDIE MERCURY

Slow Rock

Shuffle feel

Tempo I

BORN TO RUN

CLARINET

Words and Music by
BRUCE SPRINGSTEEN

D.S. al Coda

CODA

Play 3 times

BRIDGE OVER TROUBLED WATER

CLARINET

Words and Music by
PAUL SIMON

BROWN EYED GIRL

CLARINET

Words and Music by
VAN MORRISON

BROWN SUGAR

CLARINET

Words and Music by MICK JAGGER
and KEITH RICHARDS

CALIFORNIA DREAMIN'

CLARINET

Words and Music by JOHN PHILLIPS
and MICHELLE PHILLIPS

CALIFORNIA GIRLS

Clarinet

Words and Music by BRIAN WILSON
and MIKE LOVE

CRAZY

Words and Music by
WILLIE NELSON

CLARINET

A DAY IN THE LIFE

CLARINET

Words and Music by JOHN LENNON
and PAUL McCARTNEY

Tempo I

DREAM ON

CLARINET

Words and Music by
STEVEN TYLER

EVERY BREATH YOU TAKE

CLARINET

Music and Lyrics by
STING

FIRE AND RAIN

CLARINET

Words and Music by
JAMES TAYLOR

Fine

D.S. al Fine

FOR WHAT IT'S WORTH

CLARINET

Words and Music by
STEPHEN STILLS

FREE BIRD

Clarinet

Words and Music by ALLEN COLLINS
and RONNIE VAN ZANT

GIMME SOME LOVIN'

CLARINET

Words and Music by STEVE WINWOOD,
MUFF WINWOOD and SPENCER DAVIS

GLORIA

CLARINET

Words and Music by
VAN MORRISON

GOD ONLY KNOWS

Clarinet

Words and Music by BRIAN WILSON
and TONY ASHER

GOOD GOLLY MISS MOLLY

CLARINET

Words and Music by ROBERT BLACKWELL
and JOHN MARASCALCO

GOOD VIBRATIONS

CLARINET

Words and Music by BRIAN WILSON
and MIKE LOVE

GREAT BALLS OF FIRE

CLARINET

Words and Music by JACK HAMMER
and OTIS BLACKWELL

A HARD DAY'S NIGHT

Clarinet

Words and Music by JOHN LENNON
and PAUL McCARTNEY

HEARTBREAK HOTEL

CLARINET

Words and Music by MAE BOREN AXTON,
TOMMY DURDEN and ELVIS PRESLEY

HEY JUDE

CLARINET

Words and Music by JOHN LENNON
and PAUL McCARTNEY

HOTEL CALIFORNIA

Clarinet

Words and Music by DON HENLEY,
GLENN FREY and DON FELDER

HOUND DOG

Clarinet

Words and Music by JERRY LEIBER
and MIKE STOLLER

(I Can't Get No)
SATISFACTION

CLARINET

Words and Music by MICK JAGGER
and KEITH RICHARDS

I GOT YOU
(I Feel Good)

Clarinet

Words and Music by
JAMES BROWN

I HEARD IT THROUGH THE GRAPEVINE

CLARINET

Words and Music by NORMAN J. WHITFIELD
and BARRETT STRONG

I WANT TO HOLD YOUR HAND

Clarinet

Words and Music by JOHN LENNON
and PAUL McCARTNEY

IMAGINE

CLARINET

Words and Music by
JOHN LENNON

IN THE MIDNIGHT HOUR

Clarinet

Words and Music by STEVE CROPPER
and WILSON PICKETT

JAILHOUSE ROCK

Clarinet

Words and Music by JERRY LEIBER
and MIKE STOLLER

JUMP

Clarinet

Words and Music by EDWARD VAN HALEN,
ALEX VAN HALEN and DAVID LEE ROTH

LA BAMBA

CLARINET

By RITCHIE VALENS

LAYLA

CLARINET

Words and Music by ERIC CLAPTON
and JIM GORDON

LET IT BE

CLARINET

Words and Music by JOHN LENNON
and PAUL McCARTNEY

LET'S STAY TOGETHER

Clarinet

Words and Music by AL GREEN,
WILLIE MITCHELL and AL JACKSON, JR.

LIGHT MY FIRE

CLARINET

Words and Music by
THE DOORS

LIKE A ROLLING STONE

Clarinet

Words and Music by
BOB DYLAN

Moderately

LONDON CALLING

CLARINET

Words and Music by JOE STRUMMER,
MICK JONES, PAUL SIMONON
and TOPPER HEADON

LOUIE, LOUIE

CLARINET

Words and Music by
RICHARD BERRY

MAGGIE MAY

CLARINET

Words and Music by ROD STEWART
and MARTIN QUITTENTON

MORE THAN A FEELING

Clarinet

Words and Music by
TOM SCHOLZ

MY GENERATION

CLARINET

Words and Music by
PETER TOWNSHEND

MY GIRL

Clarinet

Words and Music by WILLIAM "SMOKEY" ROBINSON
and RONALD WHITE

NO WOMAN NO CRY

CLARINET

Words and Music by
VINCENT FORD

PAPA WAS A ROLLING STONE

Clarinet

Words and Music by NORMAN WHITFIELD
and BARRETT STRONG

OH, PRETTY WOMAN

Clarinet

Words and Music by ROY ORBISON
and BILL DEES

PIANO MAN

CLARINET

Words and Music by
BILLY JOEL

PROUD MARY

CLARINET

Words and Music by
JOHN FOGERTY

PURPLE HAZE

CLARINET

Words and Music by
JIMI HENDRIX

RESPECT

CLARINET

Words and Music by
OTIS REDDING

Moderately

ROCK AROUND THE CLOCK

Clarinet

Words and Music by MAX C. FREEDMAN
and JIMMY DeKNIGHT

ROXANNE

CLARINET

Music and Lyrics by
STING

SEXUAL HEALING

CLARINET

Words and Music by MARVIN GAYE,
ODELL BROWN and DAVID RITZ

SHE LOVES YOU

CLARINET

Words and Music by JOHN LENNON
and PAUL McCARTNEY

(SITTIN' ON) THE DOCK OF THE BAY

CLARINET

Words and Music by STEVE CROPPER
and OTIS REDDING

SMELLS LIKE TEEN SPIRIT

CLARINET

Words and Music by KURT COBAIN,
KRIST NOVOSELIC and DAVE GROHL

SOMEBODY TO LOVE

CLARINET

Words and Music by
DARBY SLICK

SPACE ODDITY

CLARINET

Words and Music by
DAVID BOWIE

STAIRWAY TO HEAVEN

CLARINET

Words and Music by JIMMY PAGE
and ROBERT PLANT

STAND BY ME

CLARINET

Words and Music by JERRY LEIBER,
MIKE STOLLER and BEN E. KING

START ME UP

CLARINET

Words and Music by MICK JAGGER
and KEITH RICHARDS

STRAWBERRY FIELDS FOREVER

Clarinet

Words and Music by JOHN LENNON
and PAUL McCARTNEY

STAYIN' ALIVE

CLARINET

Words and Music by BARRY GIBB,
ROBIN GIBB and MAURICE GIBB

SUITE: JUDY BLUE EYES

CLARINET

Words and Music by
STEPHEN STILLS

SUMMERTIME BLUES

CLARINET

Words and Music by EDDIE COCHRAN
and JERRY CAPEHART

SUNSHINE OF YOUR LOVE

Clarinet

Words and Music by ERIC CLAPTON,
JACK BRUCE and PETE BROWN

SUPERSTITION

CLARINET

Words and Music by
STEVIE WONDER

TANGLED UP IN BLUE

CLARINET

Words and Music by
BOB DYLAN

THAT'LL BE THE DAY

CLARINET

Words and Music by JERRY ALLISON,
NORMAN PETTY and BUDDY HOLLY

THUNDER ROAD

CLARINET

Words and Music by
BRUCE SPRINGSTEEN

THE TWIST

CLARINET

Words and Music by
HANK BALLARD

TWIST AND SHOUT

Clarinet

Words and Music by BERT RUSSELL
and PHIL MEDLEY

WALK THIS WAY

Clarinet

Words and Music by STEVEN TYLER
and JOE PERRY

WE ARE THE CHAMPIONS

Clarinet

Words and Music by
FREDDIE MERCURY

WE'VE ONLY JUST BEGUN

CLARINET

Words and Music by ROGER NICHOLS
and PAUL WILLIAMS

WHAT'D I SAY

Words and Music by
RAY CHARLES

CLARINET

WHAT'S GOING ON

CLARINET

Words and Music by RENALDO BENSON,
ALFRED CLEVELAND and MARVIN GAYE

WHEN DOVES CRY

CLARINET

Words and Music by
PRINCE

WHOLE LOTTA LOVE

Words and Music by JIMMY PAGE,
ROBERT PLANT, JOHN PAUL JONES,
JOHN BONHAM and WILLIE DIXON

Clarinet

WILD THING

CLARINET

Words and Music by
CHIP TAYLOR

WON'T GET FOOLED AGAIN

CLARINET

Words and Music by
PETER TOWNSHEND

YESTERDAY

CLARINET

Words and Music by JOHN LENNON
and PAUL McCARTNEY

Moderately

YOU REALLY GOT ME

CLARINET

Words and Music by
RAY DAVIES

YOU SHOOK ME ALL NIGHT LONG

CLARINET

Words and Music by ANGUS YOUNG,
MALCOLM YOUNG and BRIAN JOHNSON

YOUR SONG

CLARINET

Words and Music by
ELTON JOHN and BERNIE TAUPIN